The Key Facts™ on

South Africa

Essential Information on South Africa

By Patrick W. Nee

The Internationalist®
www.internationalist.com

The Internationalist®
International Business, Investment, and Travel
Published by:
The Internationalist Publishing Company
96 Walter Street/ Suite 200
Boston, MA 02131, USA
Tel: 617-354-7722
www.internationalist.com
PN@internationalist.com

Copyright © 2014 by PWN

The Internationalist is a Registered Trademark. "Key Facts" and "The Internationalist Business Guides" are Trademarks of The Internationalist Publishing Company.

All Rights are reserved under International, Pan-American, and Pan-Asian Conventions. No part of this book may be reproduced in any form without the written permission of the publisher. All rights vigorously enforced

Table Of Contents

Chapter 1: Background

Chapter 2: Geography

Chapter 3: People and Society

Chapter 4: Government and Key Leaders

Chapter 5: Economy

Chapter 6: Energy

Chapter 7: Communications

Chapter 8: Transportation

Chapter 9: Military

Chapter 10: Transnational Issues

Map of South Africa

Chapter 1: Background

Dutch traders landed at the southern tip of modern day South Africa in 1652 and established a stopover point on the spice route between the Netherlands and the Far East, founding the city of Cape Town. After the British seized the Cape of Good Hope area in 1806, many of the Dutch settlers (the Boers) trekked north to found their own republics. The discovery of diamonds (1867) and gold (1886) spurred wealth and immigration and intensified the subjugation of the native inhabitants. The Boers resisted British encroachments but were defeated in the Boer War (1899-1902); however, the British and the Afrikaners, as the Boers became known, ruled together beginning in 1910 under the Union of South Africa, which became a republic in 1961 after a whites-only referendum. In 1948, the National Party was voted into power and instituted a policy of apartheid - the separate development of the races - which favored the white minority at the expense of the black majority. The African National Congress (ANC) led the opposition to apartheid and many top ANC leaders, such as Nelson MANDELA, spent decades in South Africa's prisons. Internal protests and insurgency, as well as boycotts by some Western nations and institutions, led to the regime's eventual willingness to negotiate a peaceful transition to majority rule. The first multi-racial elections in 1994 brought an end to apartheid and ushered in majority rule under an ANC-led government. South Africa since then has struggled to address apartheid-era imbalances in decent housing, education, and health care. ANC infighting, which has grown in recent years, came to a head in September 2008 when President Thabo MBEKI resigned, and Kgalema MOTLANTHE, the party's General-Secretary, succeeded him as interim president. Jacob ZUMA became president after the ANC won general elections in April 2009.

Chapter 2: Geography

Location:
Southern Africa, at the southern tip of the continent of Africa
Geographic coordinates:
29 00 S, 24 00 E
Map references:
Africa
Area:
total: 1,219,090 sq km
country comparison to the world: 25
land: 1,214,470 sq km
water: 4,620 sq km
note: includes Prince Edward Islands (Marion Island and Prince Edward Island)
Area - comparative:
slightly less than twice the size of Texas
Land boundaries:
total: 4,862 km
border countries: Botswana 1,840 km, Lesotho 909 km, Mozambique 491 km, Namibia 967 km, Swaziland 430 km, Zimbabwe 225 km
Coastline:
2,798 km
Maritime claims:
territorial sea: 12 nm
contiguous zone: 24 nm
exclusive economic zone: 200 nm
continental shelf: 200 nm or to edge of the continental margin
Climate:
mostly semiarid; subtropical along east coast; sunny days, cool nights
Terrain:
vast interior plateau rimmed by rugged hills and narrow coastal plain

Elevation extremes:
  lowest point: Atlantic Ocean 0 m
  highest point: Njesuthi 3,408 m
Natural resources:
  gold, chromium, antimony, coal, iron ore, manganese, nickel, phosphates, tin, rare earth elements, uranium, gem diamonds, platinum, copper, vanadium, salt, natural gas
Land use:
  arable land: 9.87%
  permanent crops: 0.34%
  other: 89.79% (2011)
Irrigated land:
  16,700 sq km (2012)
Total renewable water resources:
  51.4 cu km (2011)
Freshwater withdrawal (domestic/industrial/agricultural):
  total: 12.5 cu km/yr (36%/7%/57%)
  per capita: 271.7 cu m/yr (2005)
Natural hazards:
  prolonged droughts
  volcanism: the volcano forming Marion Island in the Prince Edward Islands, which last erupted in 2004, is South Africa's only active volcano
Environment - current issues:
  lack of important arterial rivers or lakes requires extensive water conservation and control measures; growth in water usage outpacing supply; pollution of rivers from agricultural runoff and urban discharge; air pollution resulting in acid rain; soil erosion; desertification
Environment - international agreements:
  party to: Antarctic-Environmental Protocol, Antarctic-Marine Living Resources, Antarctic Seals, Antarctic Treaty, Biodiversity, Climate Change, Climate Change-Kyoto Protocol, Desertification, Endangered Species, Hazardous Wastes, Law of the Sea,

Marine Dumping, Marine Life Conservation, Ozone Layer Protection, Ship Pollution, Wetlands, Whaling

signed, but not ratified: none of the selected agreements

Geography - note:

South Africa completely surrounds Lesotho and almost completely surrounds Swaziland

Chapter 3: People and Society

Nationality:
noun: South African(s)
adjective: South African
Ethnic groups:
black African 79%, white 9.6%, colored 8.9%, Indian/Asian 2.5% (2001 census)
Languages:
IsiZulu (official) 23.82%, IsiXhosa (official) 17.64%, Afrikaans (official) 13.35%, Sepedi (offcial) 9.39%, English (official) 8.2%, Setswana (official) 8.2%, Sesotho (official) 7.93%, Xitsonga (official) 4.44%, siSwati (official) 2.66%, Tshivenda (official) 2.28%, isiNdebele (official) 1.59%, other 0.5% (2001 census)
Religions:
Protestant 36.6% (Zionist Christian 11.1%, Pentecostal/Charismatic 8.2%, Methodist 6.8%, Dutch Reformed 6.7%, Anglican 3.8%), Catholic 7.1%, Muslim 1.5%, other Christian 36%, other 2.3%, unspecified 1.4%, none 15.1% (2001 census)
Population:
48,601,098 (July 2013 est.)
country comparison to the world: 26
note: estimates for this country explicitly take into account the effects of excess mortality due to AIDS; this can result in lower life expectancy, higher infant mortality, higher death rates, lower population growth rates, and changes in the distribution of population by age and sex than would otherwise be expected
Age structure:
0-14 years: 28.3% (male 6,909,066/female 6,866,163)
15-24 years: 20.6% (male 5,041,412/female 4,960,190)
25-54 years: 38.1% (male 9,561,452/female 8,948,398)
55-64 years: 6.9% (male 1,450,420/female 1,916,960)
65 years and over: 6.1% (male 1,177,999/female 1,769,038) (2013 est.)
Median age:
total: 25.5 years

male: 25.2 years

female: 25.8 years (2013 est.)

Population growth rate:

-0.45% (2013 est.)

country comparison to the world: 221

Birth rate:

19.14 births/1,000 population (2013 est.)

country comparison to the world: 93

Death rate:

17.36 deaths/1,000 population (2013 est.)

country comparison to the world: 1

Net migration rate:

-6.24 migrant(s)/1,000 population

country comparison to the world: 196

note: there is an increasing flow of Zimbabweans into South Africa and Botswana in search of better economic opportunities (2013 est.)

Urbanization:

urban population: 62% of total population (2010)

rate of urbanization: 1.2% annual rate of change (2010-15 est.)

Major cities - population:

Johannesburg 3.607 million; Cape Town 3.353 million; Ekurhuleni (East Rand) 3.144 million; Durban 2.837 million; PRETORIA (capital) 1.404 million (2009)

Sex ratio:

at birth: 1.02 male(s)/female

0-14 years: 1.01 male(s)/female

15-24 years: 1.03 male(s)/female

25-54 years: 1.07 male(s)/female

55-64 years: 0.76 male(s)/female

65 years and over: 0.67 male(s)/female

total population: 0.99 male(s)/female (2013 est.)

Maternal mortality rate:

300 deaths/100,000 live births (2010)

country comparison to the world: 40

Infant mortality rate:

total: 42.15 deaths/1,000 live births

country comparison to the world: 52

male: 45.9 deaths/1,000 live births

female: 38.33 deaths/1,000 live births (2013 est.)

Life expectancy at birth:

total population: 49.48 years

country comparison to the world: 222

male: 50.43 years

female: 48.51 years (2013 est.)

Total fertility rate:

2.25 children born/woman (2013 est.)

country comparison to the world: 100

Health expenditures:

8.9% of GDP (2010)

country comparison to the world: 46

Physicians density:

0.77 physicians/1,000 population (2004)

Hospital bed density:

2.84 beds/1,000 population (2005)

Drinking water source:

improved:

urban: 99% of population

rural: 79% of population

total: 91% of population

unimproved:

urban: 1% of population

rural: 21% of population

total: 9% of population (2010 est.)

Sanitation facility access:
improved:
urban: 86% of population
rural: 67% of population
total: 79% of population
unimproved:
urban: 14% of population
rural: 33% of population
total: 21% of population (2010 est.)

HIV/AIDS - adult prevalence rate:
17.8% (2009 est.)
country comparison to the world: 4

HIV/AIDS - people living with HIV/AIDS:
5.6 million (2009 est.)
country comparison to the world: 1

HIV/AIDS - deaths:
310,000 (2009 est.)
country comparison to the world: 1

Major infectious diseases:
degree of risk: intermediate
food or waterborne diseases: bacterial diarrhea, hepatitis A, and typhoid fever
water contact disease: schistosomiasis (2009)

Obesity - adult prevalence rate:
31.3% (2008)
country comparison to the world: 24

Children under the age of 5 years underweight:
11.6% (2005)
country comparison to the world: 63

Education expenditures:
6% of GDP (2010)
country comparison to the world: 38

Literacy:

definition: age 15 and over can read and write

total population: 86.4%

male: 87%

female: 85.7% (2003 est.)

School life expectancy (primary to tertiary education):

total: 13 years

male: 13 years

female: 13 years (2004)

Unemployment, youth ages 15-24:

total: 49.8%

country comparison to the world: 5

male: 45.4%

female: 55% (2011)

Chapter 4: Government and Key Leaders

Country name:
conventional long form: Republic of South Africa
conventional short form: South Africa
former: Union of South Africa
abbreviation: RSA

Government type:
republic

Capital:
name: Pretoria (administrative capital)
geographic coordinates: 25 42 S, 28 13 E
time difference: UTC+2 (7 hours ahead of Washington, DC during Standard Time)
note: Cape Town (legislative capital); Bloemfontein (judicial capital)

Administrative divisions:
9 provinces; Eastern Cape, Free State, Gauteng, KwaZulu-Natal, Limpopo, Mpumalanga, Northern Cape, North-West, Western Cape

Independence:
31 May 1910 (Union of South Africa formed from four British colonies: Cape Colony, Natal, Transvaal, and Orange Free State); 31 May 1961 (republic declared); 27 April 1994 (majority rule)

National holiday:
Freedom Day, 27 April (1994)

Constitution:
10 December 1996; note - certified by the Constitutional Court 4 December 1996; was signed by then President MANDELA 10 December 1996; and entered into effect 4 February 1997

Legal system:
mixed legal system of Roman-Dutch civil law, English common law, and customary law

International law organization participation:
has not submitted an ICJ jurisdiction declaration; accepts ICCt jurisdiction

Suffrage:

18 years of age; universal

Executive branch:

chief of state: President Jacob ZUMA (since 9 May 2009); Deputy President Kgalema MOTLANTHE (since 11 May 2009); note - the president is both the chief of state and head of government

head of government: President Jacob ZUMA (since 9 May 2009); Deputy President Kgalema MOTLANTHE (since 11 May 2009)

cabinet: Cabinet appointed by the president

elections: president elected by the National Assembly for a five-year term (eligible for a second term); election last held on 6 May 2009 (next to be held in 2014)

election results: Jacob ZUMA elected president; National Assembly vote - Jacob ZUMA 277, Mvume DANDALA 47, other 76

Legislative branch:

bicameral Parliament consisting of the National Council of Provinces (90 seats; 10 members elected by each of the nine provincial legislatures for five-year terms; has special powers to protect regional interests, including the safeguarding of cultural and linguistic traditions among ethnic minorities) and the National Assembly (400 seats; members elected by popular vote under a system of proportional representation to serve five-year terms)

elections: National Assembly and National Council of Provinces - last held on 22 April 2009 (next to be held in April 2014)

election results: National Council of Provinces - percent of vote by party - NA; seats by party - NA; National Assembly - percent of vote by party - ANC 65.9%, DA 16.7%, COPE 7.4%, IFP 4.6%, other 5.4%; seats by party - ANC 264, DA 67, COPE 30, IFP 18, other 21

Judicial branch:

Constitutional Court; Supreme Court of Appeals; High Courts; Magistrate Courts

Political parties and leaders:

African Christian Democratic Party or ACDP [Kenneth MESHOE]; African National Congress or ANC [Jacob ZUMA]; Congress of the People or COPE [Mosiuoa LEKOTA];

Democratic Alliance or DA [Helen ZILLE]; Freedom Front Plus or FF+ [Pieter MULDER]; Inkatha Freedom Party or IFP [Mangosuthu BUTHELEZI]; Pan-Africanist Congress or PAC [Motsoko PHEKO]; United Christian Democratic Party or UCDP [Lucas MANGOPE]; United Democratic Movement or UDM [Bantu HOLOMISA]

Political pressure groups and leaders:

Congress of South African Trade Unions or COSATU [Zwelinzima VAVI, general secretary]; South African Communist Party or SACP [Blade NZIMANDE, general secretary]; South African National Civics Organization or SANCO [Mlungisi HLONGWANE, national president]

note: COSATU and SACP are in a formal alliance with the ANC

International organization participation:

ACP, AfDB, AU, BIS, BRICS, C, CD, FAO, FATF, G-20, G-24, G-77, IAEA, IBRD, ICAO, ICC (national committees), ICRM, IDA, IFAD, IFC, IFRCS, IHO, ILO, IMF, IMO, IMSO, Interpol, IOC, IOM, IPU, ISO, ITSO, ITU, ITUC (NGOs), MIGA, MONUSCO, NAM, NSG, OECD (Enhanced Engagement, OPCW, Paris Club (associate), PCA, SACU, SADC, UN, UNAMID, UNCTAD, UNESCO, UNHCR, UNIDO, UNITAR, UNSC (temporary), UNWTO, UPU, WCO, WFTU (NGOs), WHO, WIPO, WMO, WTO, ZC

Diplomatic representation in the US:

chief of mission: Ambassador Ebrahim RASOOL
chancery: 3051 Massachusetts Avenue NW, Washington, DC 20008
telephone: [1] (202) 232-4400
FAX: [1] (202) 265-1607
consulate(s) general: Chicago, Los Angeles, New York

Diplomatic representation from the US:

chief of mission: Ambassador Donald H. GIPS
embassy: 877 Pretorius Street, Pretoria
mailing address: P. O. Box 9536, Pretoria 0001
telephone: [27] (12) 431-4000
FAX: [27] (12) 342-2299
consulate(s) general: Cape Town, Durban, Johannesburg

Key Leaders

Pres.	Jacob ZUMA
Dep. Pres.	Kgalema MOTLANTHE
Min. of Agriculture, Forestry, & Fisheries	Tina JOEMAT-PETTERSSON
Min. of Arts & Culture	Paul MASHATILE
Min. of Basic Education	Matsie Angelina MOTSHEKGA
Min. of Communications	Dina Deliwe PULE
Min. of Cooperative Governance & Traditional Affairs	Richard Masenyani BALOYI
Min. of Correctional Services	Joel Sibusiso NDEBELE
Min. of Defense & Military Veterans	Nosiviwe Noluthando MAPISA-NQAKULA
Min. of Economic Development	Ebrahim PATEL
Min. of Energy	Elizabeth Dipuo PETERS
Min. of Finance	Pravin Jamnadas GORDHAN
Min. of Health	Pakishe Aaron MOTSOALEDI, *Dr.*
Min. of Higher Education & Training	Bonginkosi Emmanuel "Blade" NZIMANDE
Min. of Home Affairs	Grace Naledi Mandisa PANDOR
Min. of Human Settlements	Gabriel Mosima "Tokyo" SEXWALE

Min. of Intl. Relations & Cooperation	Maite NKOANA-MASHABANE
Min. of Justice & Constitutional Development	Jeffrey Thamsanga RADEBE
Min. of Labor	Nelisiwe Mildred OLIPHANT
Min. of Mineral Resources	Susan SHABANGU
Min. of Police	Nkosinathi Emmanuel "Nathi" MTHETHWA
Min. of Public Enterprises	Malusi Knowledge Nkanyezi GIGABA
Min. of Public Service & Admin.	Lindiwe Nonceba SISULU
Min. of Public Works	Thembelani "Thulas" NXESI
Min. of Rural Development & Land Reform	Gugile Ernest NKWINTI
Min. of Science & Technology	Derek Andre HANEKOM
Min. of Social Development	Bathabile Olive DLAMINI
Min. of Sport & Recreation	Fikile April MBALULA
Min. of State Security	Siyabonga Cyprian CWELE
Min. of Tourism	Marthinus VAN

	SCHALKWYK
Min. of Trade & Industry	Robert Haydn DAVIES
Min. of Transport	Benedict MARTINS
Min. of Water & Environmental Affairs	Bomo Edna MOLEWA
Min. of Women, Youth, Children, & People With Disabilities	Lulama "Lulu" Marytheresa XINGWANA
Min. in the Presidency - National Planning Commission	Trevor Andrew MANUEL
Min. in the Presidency - Performance Monitoring & Evaluation	Ohm Collins CHABANE
Governor, South African Reserve Bank	Gill MARCUS
Ambassador to the US	Ebrahim RASOOL
Permanent Representative to the UN, New York	Jeremiah Nyamane Kingsley MAMABOLO

Flag description:

two equal width horizontal bands of red (top) and blue separated by a central green band that splits into a horizontal Y, the arms of which end at the corners of the hoist side; the Y embraces a black isosceles triangle from which the arms are separated by narrow yellow bands; the red and blue bands are separated from the green band and its arms by narrow white stripes; the flag colors do not have any official symbolism, but the Y stands for the "convergence of diverse elements within South African society, taking the road ahead in unity"; black, yellow, and green are found on the flag of the African National Congress, while red, white, and blue are the colors in the flags of the Netherlands and the UK, whose settlers ruled South Africa during the colonial era

note: the South African flag is one of only two national flags to display six colors as part of its primary design, the other is South Sudan's

National symbol(s):
springbok antelope

National anthem:
name: "National Anthem of South Africa"

lyrics/music: Enoch SONTONGA and Cornelius Jacob LANGENHOVEN/Enoch SONTONGA and Marthinus LOURENS de Villiers

note: adopted 1994; the anthem is a combination of "N'kosi Sikelel' iAfrica" (God Bless Africa) and "Die Stem van Suid Afrika" (The Call of South Africa), which were respectively the anthems of the non-white and white communities under apartheid; the official lyrics contain a mixture of Xhosa, Zulu, Sesotho, Afrikaans, and English; the music incorporates the melody used in the Tanzanian and Zambian anthems

Chapter 5: Economy

Economy - overview:

South Africa is a middle-income, emerging market with an abundant supply of natural resources; well-developed financial, legal, communications, energy, and transport sectors and a stock exchange that is the 15th largest in the world. Even though the country possesses modern infrastructure that support a relatively efficient distribution of goods to major urban centers throughout the region, some components retard growth. The economy began to slow in the second half of 2007 due to an electricity crisis. State power supplier Eskom encountered problems with aging plants and meeting electricity demand necessitating "load-shedding" cuts in 2007 and 2008 to residents and businesses in the major cities. Subsequently, the global financial crisis reduced commodity prices and world demand. GDP fell nearly 2% in 2009 but has recovered since then. Unemployment, poverty, and inequality remain a challenge, with official unemployment at nearly 25% of the work force. State power supplier Eskom has built two new power stations and installed new power demand management programs to improve power grid reliability. South Africa's economic policy has focused on controlling inflation, however, the country has had significant budget deficits that restrict its ability to deal with pressing economic problems. The current government faces growing pressure from special interest groups to use state-owned enterprises to deliver basic services to low-income areas and to increase job growth.

GDP (purchasing power parity):
$578.6 billion (2012 est.)
country comparison to the world: 26
$564 billion (2011 est.)
$546.9 billion (2010 est.)
note: data are in 2012 US dollars

GDP (official exchange rate):
$390.9 billion (2012 est.)

GDP - real growth rate:
2.6% (2012 est.)

country comparison to the world: 125

3.1% (2011 est.)

2.9% (2010 est.)

GDP - per capita (PPP):

$11,300 (2012 est.)

country comparison to the world: 109

$11,100 (2011 est.)

$10,900 (2010 est.)

note: data are in 2012 US dollars

GDP - composition by sector:

agriculture: 2.4%

industry: 32.1%

services: 64.9% (2012 est.)

Labor force:

17.89 million (2012 est.)

country comparison to the world: 35

Labor force - by occupation:

agriculture: 9%

industry: 26%

services: 65% (2007 est.)

Unemployment rate:

22.7% (2012 est.)

country comparison to the world: 168

24.9% (2011 est.)

Population below poverty line:

31.3% (2009 est.)

Household income or consumption by percentage share:

lowest 10%: 1.2%

highest 10%: 51.7% (2009 est.)

Distribution of family income - Gini index:

63.1 (2005)

country comparison to the world: 2

59.3 (1994)

Investment (gross fixed):

20.9% of GDP (2012 est.)

country comparison to the world: 84

Budget:

revenues: $95.27 billion

expenditures: $116.5 billion (2012 est.)

Taxes and other revenues:

24.4% of GDP (2012 est.)

country comparison to the world: 128

Budget surplus (+) or deficit (-):

-5.4% of GDP (2012 est.)

country comparison to the world: 165

Public debt:

43.3% of GDP (2012 est.)

country comparison to the world: 83

38.6% of GDP (2011 est.)

Inflation rate (consumer prices):

5.2% (2012 est.)

country comparison to the world: 145

5% (2011 est.)

Central bank discount rate:

5% (31 December 2012)

country comparison to the world: 38

7% (31 December 2009)

Commercial bank prime lending rate:

8.8% (31 December 2012 est.)

country comparison to the world: 99

9% (31 December 2011 est.)

Stock of narrow money:

$117 billion (31 December 2012 est.)

country comparison to the world: 30

$117.3 billion (31 December 2011 est.)

Stock of broad money:

$277 billion (31 December 2011 est.)

country comparison to the world: 34

$314.1 billion (31 December 2010 est.)

Stock of domestic credit:

$287.9 billion (31 December 2012 est.)

country comparison to the world: 37

$284.7 billion (31 December 2011 est.)

Market value of publicly traded shares:

$1.038 trillion (31 December 2012)

country comparison to the world: 16

$855.7 billion (31 December 2011)

$1.013 trillion (31 December 2010)

Agriculture - products:

corn, wheat, sugarcane, fruits, vegetables; beef, poultry, mutton, wool, dairy products

Industries:

mining (world's largest producer of platinum, gold, chromium), automobile assembly, metalworking, machinery, textiles, iron and steel, chemicals, fertilizer, foodstuffs, commercial ship repair

Industrial production growth rate:

2.5% (2011 est.)

country comparison to the world: 103

Current account balance:

$-21.33 billion (2012 est.)

country comparison to the world: 183

$-13.68 billion (2011 est.)

Exports:

$101.2 billion (2012 est.)

country comparison to the world: 40
$102.9 billion (2011 est.)
Exports - commodities:
gold, diamonds, platinum, other metals and minerals, machinery and equipment
Exports - partners:
China 12.7%, US 8.6%, Japan 7.9%, Germany 6%, UK 4.1% (2011)
Imports:
$106.8 billion (2012 est.)
country comparison to the world: 34
$100.4 billion (2011 est.)
Imports - commodities:
machinery and equipment, chemicals, petroleum products, scientific instruments, foodstuffs
Imports - partners:
China 14.3%, Germany 10.7%, US 8%, Japan 4.7%, Saudi Arabia 4.5%, India 4%, UK 4% (2011)
Reserves of foreign exchange and gold:
$54.98 billion (31 December 2012 est.)
country comparison to the world: 34
$48.87 billion (31 December 2011 est.)
Debt - external:
$47.56 billion (31 December 2012 est.)
country comparison to the world: 59
$47.49 billion (31 December 2011 est.)
Stock of direct foreign investment - at home:
$162.9 billion (31 December 2012 est.)
country comparison to the world: 27
$158.9 billion (31 December 2011 est.)
Stock of direct foreign investment - abroad:
$88.59 billion (31 December 2012 est.)
country comparison to the world: 29

$88.95 billion (31 December 2011 est.)

Exchange rates:

rand (ZAR) per US dollar -

8.1 (2012 est.)

7.26 (2011 est.)

7.32 (2010 est.)

8.42 (2009)

7.96 (2008)

Fiscal year:

1 April - 31 March

Chapter 6: Energy

Electricity - production:
 257.9 billion kWh (2012 est.)
 country comparison to the world: 16

Electricity - consumption:
 234.2 billion kWh (2012 est.)
 country comparison to the world: 17

Electricity - exports:
 15.04 billion kWh (2012 est.)
 country comparison to the world: 12

Electricity - imports:
 10.06 billion kWh (2012 est.)
 country comparison to the world: 23

Electricity - installed generating capacity:
 44.26 million kW (2009 est.)
 country comparison to the world: 22

Electricity - from fossil fuels:
 90.8% of total installed capacity (2009 est.)
 country comparison to the world: 75

Electricity - from nuclear fuels:
 4.1% of total installed capacity (2009 est.)
 country comparison to the world: 25

Electricity - from hydroelectric plants:
 1.5% of total installed capacity (2009 est.)
 country comparison to the world: 141

Electricity - from other renewable sources:
 0.5% of total installed capacity (2009 est.)
 country comparison to the world: 76

Crude oil - production:
 169,000 bbl/day (2011 est.)

country comparison to the world: 41

Crude oil - exports:

0 bbl/day (2009 est.)

country comparison to the world: 179

Crude oil - imports:

402,300 bbl/day (2009 est.)

country comparison to the world: 22

Crude oil - proved reserves:

15 million bbl (1 January 2012 es)

country comparison to the world: 88

Refined petroleum products - production:

516,100 bbl/day (2008 est.)

country comparison to the world: 32

Refined petroleum products - consumption:

590,900 bbl/day (2011 est.)

country comparison to the world: 30

Refined petroleum products - exports:

49,430 bbl/day (2008 est.)

country comparison to the world: 60

Refined petroleum products - imports:

60,290 bbl/day (2008 est.)

country comparison to the world: 63

Natural gas - production:

970 million cu m (2010 est.)

country comparison to the world: 65

Natural gas - consumption:

4.01 billion cu m (2010 est.)

country comparison to the world: 67

Natural gas - exports:

0 cu m (2010 est.)

country comparison to the world: 175

Natural gas - imports:

3.04 billion cu m (2010 est.)

country comparison to the world: 43

Natural gas - proved reserves:

27.16 million cu m (1 January 2006 es)

country comparison to the world: 104

Carbon dioxide emissions from consumption of energy:

465.1 million Mt (2010 est.)

country comparison to the world: 13

Chapter 7: Communications

Telephones - main lines in use:
4.127 million (2011)
country comparison to the world: 42

Telephones - mobile cellular:
64 million (2011)
country comparison to the world: 20

Telephone system:
general assessment: the system is the best developed and most modern in Africa
domestic: combined fixed-line and mobile-cellular teledensity is roughly 140 telephones per 100 persons; consists of carrier-equipped open-wire lines, coaxial cables, microwave radio relay links, fiber-optic cable, radiotelephone communication stations, and wireless local loops; key centers are Bloemfontein, Cape Town, Durban, Johannesburg, Port Elizabeth, and Pretoria
international: country code - 27; the SAT-3/WASC and SAFE fiber-optic submarine cable systems connect South Africa to Europe and Asia; the EASSy fiber-optic cable system connects with Europe and North America; satellite earth stations - 3 Intelsat (1 Indian Ocean and 2 Atlantic Ocean) (2011)

Broadcast media:
the South African Broadcasting Corporation (SABC) operates 4 TV stations, 3 are free-to-air and 1 is pay TV; e.tv, a private station, is accessible to more than half the population; multiple subscription TV services provide a mix of local and international channels; well developed mix of public and private radio stations at the national, regional, and local levels; the SABC radio network, state-owned and controlled but nominally independent, operates 18 stations, one for each of the 11 official languages, 4 community stations, and 3 commercial stations; more than 100 community-based stations extend coverage to rural areas (2007)

Internet country code:
.za

Internet hosts:

4.761 million (2012)

country comparison to the world: 23

Internet users:

4.42 million (2009)

country comparison to the world: 54

Chapter 8: Transportation

Airports:

567 (2012)

country comparison to the world: 11

Airports - with paved runways:

total: 145

over 3,047 m: 11

2,438 to 3,047 m: 6

1,524 to 2,437 m: 53

914 to 1,523 m: 66

under 914 m: 9 (2012)

Airports - with unpaved runways:

total: 422

2,438 to 3,047 m: 1

1,524 to 2,437 m: 29

914 to 1,523 m: 260

under 914 m: 132 (2012)

Heliports:

1 (2012)

Pipelines:

condensate 11 km; gas 908 km; oil 980 km; refined products 1,382 km (2010)

Railways:

total: 20,192 km

country comparison to the world: 14

narrow gauge: 19,756 km 1.065-m gauge (8,271 km electrified); 122 km 0.750-m gauge; 314 km 0.610-m gauge (2008)

Roadways:

total: 362,099 km

country comparison to the world: 18

paved: 73,506 km (includes 239 km of expressways)

unpaved: 288,593 km (2002)

Merchant marine:

total: 3

country comparison to the world: 136

by type: petroleum tanker 3

registered in other countries: 19 (Australia 1, Isle of Man 2, Mexico 1, NZ 1, Seychelles 1, Singapore 13) (2010)

Ports and terminals:

Cape Town, Durban, Port Elizabeth, Richards Bay, Saldanha Bay

Chapter 9: Military

Military branches:
South African National Defense Force (SANDF): South African Army, South African Navy (SAN), South African Air Force (SAAF), Joint Operations Command, Military Intelligence, South African Military Health Services (2009)

Military service age and obligation:
18 years of age for voluntary military service; women are eligible to serve in noncombat roles; 2-year service obligation (2007)

Manpower available for military service:
males age 16-49: 13,439,781
females age 16-49: 12,473,641 (2010 est.)

Manpower fit for military service:
males age 16-49: 7,617,063
females age 16-49: 6,476,264 (2010 est.)

Manpower reaching militarily significant age annually:
male: 482,122
female: 485,017 (2010 est.)

Military expenditures:
1.7% of GDP (2006)
country comparison to the world: 87

Military - note:
with the end of apartheid and the establishment of majority rule, former military, black homelands forces, and ex-opposition forces were integrated into the South African National Defense Force (SANDF); as of 2003 the integration process was considered complete

Chapter 10: Transnational Issues

Disputes - international:

South Africa has placed military units to assist police operations along the border of Lesotho, Zimbabwe, and Mozambique to control smuggling, poaching, and illegal migration; the governments of South Africa and Namibia have not signed or ratified the text of the 1994 Surveyor's General agreement placing the boundary in the middle of the Orange River

Refugees and internally displaced persons:

refugees (country of origin): 15,186 (Somalia); 12,973 (Democratic Republic of Congo); 5,808 (Angola) (2011)

Illicit drugs:

transshipment center for heroin, hashish, and cocaine, as well as a major cultivator of marijuana in its own right; cocaine and heroin consumption on the rise; world's largest market for illicit methaqualone, usually imported illegally from India through various east African countries, but increasingly producing its own synthetic drugs for domestic consumption; attractive venue for money launderers given the increasing level of organized criminal and narcotics activity in the region and the size of the South African economy

Map of South Africa

Other Key Facts™ Titles

Key Facts on Syria

Key Facts on China

Key Facts on Qatar

Key Facts on India

Key Facts on Germany

Key Facts on Argentina

Key Facts on Russia

Key Facts on North Korea

Key Facts on Brazil

Key Facts on Italy

Key Facts on the United Arab Emirates

Key Facts on the European Union

Key Facts on Pakistan

Key Facts on Saudi Arabia

Key Facts on Cyprus

Key Facts on Iran

Key Facts on Afghanistan

Key Facts on Iraq

Key Facts on Indonesia

Key Facts on South Korea

Key Facts on France

Key Facts on the United Kingdom

Key Facts on Egypt

Key Facts on Israel

Key Facts on Mexico

Key Facts on the United States of America

Key Facts on Turkey

All Key Facts™ Titles are Available at www.Amazon.com

THE INTERNATIONALIST®
2013
WWW.INTERNATIONALIST.COM

www.ingramcontent.com/pod-product-compliance
Lightning Source LLC
Chambersburg PA
CBHW070722180526
45167CB00004B/1584